Trails to California

Ann Ingalls

Consultants

Kristina Jovin, M.A.T.
Alvord Unified School District
Teacher of the Year

Bijan Kazarooni, M.A.
Department of History
Chapman University

Publishing Credits

Rachelle Cracchiolo, M.S.Ed., *Publisher*
Conni Medina, M.A.Ed., *Managing Editor*
Emily R. Smith, M.A.Ed., *Series Developer*
June Kikuchi, *Content Director*
Marc Pioch, M.A.Ed., and Susan Daddis, M.A.Ed., *Editors*
Courtney Roberson, *Senior Graphic Designer*

Image Credits: Cover and p.1 Oil On Canvas by Bob Coronato www.BobCoronato.com; pp.2–3 Library of Congress [LC-USZ62-11012]; p.4 Time Life Pictures/National Archives/The LIFE Picture Collection/Getty Images; p.5 Library of Congress [LC-DIG-ppmsc-04818]; p.6 From family papers, first published in Maurice Sullivan, The travels of Jedediah Smith, Santa Ana, Calif., The Fine Arts Press, 1934; p.7 Library of Congress [LC-USZC4-849]; pp.8, 32 North Wind Picture Archives; p.9 National Archives and Records Administration [528114]; p.10 Library of Congress [LC-DIG-pga-07709]; pp.10–11 Library of Congress [LC-DIG-pga-03551]; p.11 (top) Library of Congress [LC-DIG-highsm-23831]; p.12 Glasshouse Images/Newscom; pp.12–13 Library of Congress [LC-USZ62-123305]; pp.14–15 Creative Commons Attribution-Share Alike 3.0 Unported by Famartin; pp.15 (top), 23 Granger, NYC; pp.15 (bottom), 17 ABN IMAGES/Alamy Stock Photo; p.16 Sutter's Fort State Historic Park Archives in Sacramento; pp.18–19 Grass Valley, Nevada County, California, Robert B. Honeyman, Jr. collection of early Californian and Western American pictorial material [graphic], BANC PIC 1963.002:0862--D. Courtesy of The Bancroft Library, University of California, Berkeley; p.19 (top) The Shirley Letters from California Mines in 1851-52: being a series of twenty-three letters from Dame Shirley; p.20 Creative Commons Attribution-Share Alike 4.0 International by Wikicuda; p.21 Humboldt Room collection #2003.01.0773, Humboldt State University; pp.22–23 Creative Commons Attribution-Share Alike 3.0 Unported by Fredlyfish4; p.24 (bottom) Library of Congress [g4051s.ct000909]; p.25 (top) Creative Commons Attribution-Share Alike 3.0 Unported by Zandcee; p.25 (full page) Don Graham, Redlands, CA https://www.flickr.com/photos/23155134@N06/; pp.26–27 Library of Congress [LC-DIG-pga-02904]; p.27 AP Photo/Rich Pedroncelli; p.28 Time Life Pictures/National Archives/The LIFE Picture Collection/Getty Images; p.29 (top) Library of Congress [LC-DIG-det-4a20715], (bottom) Library of Congress [LC-DIG-ppmsc-02506]; pp.31, back cover ABN IMAGES/Alamy Stock Photo; all other images from iStock and/or Shutterstock.

Library of Congress Cataloging-in-Publication Data
Names: Ingalls, Ann, author.
Title: Trails to California / Ann Ingalls.
Description: Huntington Beach, CA : Teacher Created Materials, Inc., 2017. | Includes index.
Identifiers: LCCN 2017014100 (print) | LCCN 2017025144 (ebook) | ISBN 9781425835071 (eBook) | ISBN 9781425832377 (pbk.)
Subjects: LCSH: West (U.S.)--History--To 1848--Juvenile literature. | West (U.S.)--History--1848-1860--Juvenile literature. | Overland journeys to the Pacific--Juvenile literature. | Frontier and pioneer life--West (U.S.)--Juvenile literature. | Pioneers--West (U.S.)--History--19th century--Juvenile literature. | California National Historic Trail--Juvenile literature.
Classification: LCC F592 (ebook) | LCC F592 .I57 2017 (print) | DDC 978/.02--dc23
LC record available at https://lccn.loc.gov/2017014100

Teacher Created Materials
5301 Oceanus Drive
Huntington Beach, CA 92649-1030
http://www.tcmpub.com

ISBN 978-1-4258-3237-7

Table of Contents

Trails West

By the mid-1800s, people began to venture west in search of new lives. Men, women, and children sometimes traveled up to 2,000 miles (3,219 kilometers) in hopes of claiming land and riches. **Trappers** and traders had explored some of these lands before. But now, entire families packed into wagons for long journeys.

Trips to the West were harsh. People often had to travel through **passes**, over high mountains, and across dry deserts. Many of them faced hunger, cold, and **fatigue** along the way. At the end of each day, guides chose places to camp. People slept in tents, in wagons, or on the ground under the stars.

The journey was hard, but if the travelers could make it to the end of the trail, they had a chance at better lives. As more people went west, forts and new **industries** rose up. Some people formed settlements there. Women had new **prospects** that they did not have back home. All these people helped map the West for future generations.

This 1865 covered wagon is full of clothes and other belongings to make the trip west.

Murphy Wagons

Joseph Murphy made the most well-known wagons used to go west. He started his business in 1825. His wagons were large and strongly built. They were 9 feet (2.7 meters) high and 12 feet (3.7 meters) long. Travelers used oxen to pull these wagons for the long journeys.

California Trail

The California Trail was about 2,000 miles (3,219 kilometers) long. The exact length was based on where people started and ended their trips. Most people left to go west in April or May. Starting at this time helped them cross the Sierra Nevada before the snow made it impossible to cross the mountains.

Geography

This drawing shows part of the California Trail in 1859.

Trappers and Traders

Before the Gold Rush in 1849, there was another rush in California. Trappers and traders came in large numbers to the land for the Fur Rush. They wanted to get rich by selling valuable furs. Mammals, such as otters, foxes, and seals, were hunted for their furs.

Jedediah Smith

Of all the trappers in the early years, an American trapper was one of the best. His name was Jedediah Strong Smith. Like many mountain men, Smith went west to make money. While working as a guide in the winter of 1823, he camped with a group of Crow Indians. They told him of a pass through the Rocky Mountains.

Three years later, Smith led another group west. They crossed the South Pass that Smith had learned about from the Crow Indians. The people in this group became the first Americans from the east to enter California over land. Smith had proven that the South Pass was the best way to get to the West Coast. After Smith's trip, the South Pass became one of the most widely used routes for people heading west.

Narrow Escape

Smith lived through dozens of narrow escapes. He was attacked by a grizzly bear in the Black Hills but still continued westward.

Jedediah Smith

An Early End

Smith became a trader when he was 31 years old. He faced danger while exploring and trapping, but it was while he was trading that he met his death. In 1831, Smith led a group along the Santa Fe Trail to search for water. Comanche (kuh-MAN-chee) warriors surrounded the group and killed Smith.

Smith leads a group across the Mojave Desert in 1826.

Columbia R.

Walla Walla

Snake R.

The Oregon Trail

Fort Boise

Fort Ha

Fort Bridger

Great
Salt Lake

Salt L

The California Trail

Humboldt R.

Sacramento R.

Sacramento

San Francisco

Trail

TheSpani

Colorado R.

So

M

The Lucky Ones

Bidwell's group started with 69 people.
Only 32 men, 1 woman, and 1 baby
survived the whole trip. They were the
first group to travel by land on what would
become known as the California Trail. But
by the end, they couldn't claim to be the
first wagon train. They had lost all the
wagons along the way.

San Pedro

John Bidwell

John Bidwell led one of the first groups of **emigrants** from the Missouri River to California. Bidwell and his **party** left Missouri in May 1841. They started out on the Oregon Trail. At one point, they made a left turn and were on the California Trail. No one in the group had ever taken this route.

There were many struggles along the way. When wagons stalled in the mud or got caught on tall grass, people had to leave behind some of their goods. They crossed unsafe rivers, canyons, cliffs, and **gulches**. Some days, they only traveled 12 miles (19 kilometers).

Finding fresh water and a steady food supply was hard. People began to kill the pack animals for food. Finally, they reached the first settlement after crossing the Sierra Nevada. There, they found food, clothing, and shelter. Once the group was settled, Bidwell went looking for work. A man named John Sutter said he could use Bidwell's help as a business manager for his fort. Bidwell later found gold and became a wealthy man.

An Educator

Bidwell was born in New York in 1819. His family moved to Ohio 12 years later. Education was important to him. When he was 17, Bidwell walked 300 miles (483 kilometers) through snow so that he could attend school away from home. The next year, he was made principal of the school.

John Bidwell

Sutter's Fort

In 1839, John Sutter fled major **debt** in Switzerland and went to California. Once there, he became a Mexican citizen so he could get a land grant. He called his land *Nueva Helvetia* (NWAY-vuh hel-VEE-shuh). He built Sutter's Fort on this land. Two years later, he bought Fort Ross from Russian settlers. Sutter moved livestock, tools, and buildings from Fort Ross to Sutter's Fort.

Travelers were pleased when they found Sutter's Fort. That meant they were almost at the end of the trail. Traders, trappers, and settlers found jobs there. One of those travelers was John Bidwell. When he arrived at the fort, Sutter hired him as **caretaker**. American Indians worked there, too. Sutter paid them very little for their hard work, but the fact that he paid them at all was **radical** for the time.

Sutter's success came to an end in 1848. One of his workers found gold. When Sutter saw it, he wanted everyone on the fort to stay quiet. Instead, word got out that there was gold on his land. People rushed to his land, stole his goods, and killed his livestock. By 1852, Sutter was ruined.

John Sutter

A mill on Sutter's Fort was rebuilt to show how it looked during the Gold Rush.

Jobs at the Fort

Farming became a large operation at Sutter's Fort. The residents grew peas, cotton, wheat, and other crops. They also kept thousands of cattle and sheep on hand. Inside the fort, workers made blankets and baked bread, among other jobs.

Sutter's Fort

James Beckwourth

Life as a mountain man was risky. James Beckwourth, an African American, was one of the best. He was born into slavery in 1798. He gained his freedom in 1810 with help from his father. Beckwourth began living with the Crow Indians in 1828. He learned their language and studied their **customs**. The tribe even named him a chief. For the next two decades, he did many jobs. He worked as a scout, a trader, and an innkeeper.

In 1851, Beckwourth led the first wagon train into Marysville, California. He discovered what is called *Beckwourth Pass*. The trail, which was also named for him, was widely used for travel for about four years. At that time, the railroad became more popular for travel from coast to coast.

In 1864, Beckwourth went back to the Crow village. He died two years later. The details of his death are unknown. Some **historians** believe he was placed on a tree platform after he died. This was how the Crow tribes honored their dead.

An Imposing Figure

Beckwourth was 6 feet (1.8 meters) tall and known for being incredibly strong. He often wore his hair to his waist, sometimes in braids. He wore ribbons, earrings, gold chains, and Crow leggings. A bullet hung from a cord around his neck.

three members of
the Crow tribe

Fleeting Fame

In 1856, Beckwourth told his life story to Thomas D. Bonner. Bonner wrote a book. It was printed in French in 1860. For a time, it earned Beckwourth some fame. The book is the only record of an African American's life in the West at this time in history.

This is Hastings Cutoff, where the Donner Party mistakenly turned.

The Donner Party

On April 16, 1846, George and Jacob Donner packed their families into nine covered wagons. They were headed to new lives in California. A guide named Lansford Hastings had written about a shortcut the Donner men wanted to take. But Hastings **underestimated** how hard the route would be. Once Hastings tried his shortcut, it became clear that the route was too hard to take. So, Hastings left notes that sent the group a different way. It was a disaster! It cost them 18 days.

Finally, they reached the Sierra Nevada range. When they got there, they saw that snow blocked the route. The party was forced to spend five months in **crude** tents and cabins with very little food. The group sent 15 men to find help. Eight of those men died before reaching a ranch in California. The remaining seven made it to a safe place. They told how the Donner Party was stranded.

It took more than two months to rescue the rest of the Donner Party. By then, almost half of them had died. It is rumored that some of the people left in the mountains resorted to **cannibalism**.

Young Travelers

About a month into the Donners' journey, they joined another large wagon train. After that, there were 87 people in the Donner Party. More than half of them were under the age of 18. Isabella Breen, who was one year old at the time, survived the trip. When she died in 1935, she was the last survivor of the Donner Party.

The Pioneer Monument

In Truckee, California, a statue honors members of the Donner Party. It is located at the site where the Donner Party was stuck for the winter. The base of the monument is 22 feet (6.7 meters) high. This height is to show how deep the snow was for the travelers.

This monument to the Donner Party was placed at the site of the Donner camp in 1928.

John Stark, Rescuer

Word spread that the Donner Party needed help. In all, there were four rescue attempts. During one of the attempts, one man stood out from the rest.

John Stark was part of the third rescue party. On the way to the mountains, his party met up with 11 survivors who had been left behind in an earlier rescue attempt. They were **huddled** around a fire at the bottom of a deep snow pit. All of them were too weak to walk. The rescuers planned to take only four people. They told everyone else that they would have to wait. Stark refused. "I will not abandon these people."

Stark encouraged the tired adults to keep going and gathered the children. He took two at a time for a few yards, set them down, and went back to get the others. Because of Stark, all 11 people made it out of the snow pit alive.

Stark Appreciation

James Breen was one of the children who Stark helped rescue. Later in life, he spoke about what Stark meant to him. "To his great bodily strength, and **unexcelled** courage, myself and others owe our lives."

John Stark

Sutter Helps

Sutter helped support one rescue **mission** for the stranded Donner Party in November. It was not successful. Finally, on the third try, he opened his fort to the 45 survivors. They were allowed to stay until their health was restored.

Donner Pass, in the Sierra Nevada, is where the Donner Party was blocked by snow.

Women in the West

Along with men, women faced the harsh realities of life on the trails. However, settlements also offered women new opportunities. Building new lives in the West allowed women more independence from men.

Sarah Royce

"No house was within sight," Sarah Royce wrote in her diary about her first day on the trail. "Why did I look for one?" She, her husband, and their baby girl headed west as part of a wagon train. Josiah Royce wanted to get rich during the Gold Rush. Traveling over land was a long, hard journey.

They made it to California in the fall of 1849. At the first mine, the couple did not find any gold. Instead, they opened a store with supplies. They moved several times before settling in Grass Valley. There, they had three more children. Sarah was a little nervous about being in mining camps. But she quickly learned that her fears could be put aside. The other men in the camp looked out for her and her children.

Journey Journal

Josiah Royce Jr. became a famous historian. As an adult, he wrote a book about the state's history. He asked his mother to revise her journal so he could use it. She changed some parts of her original writings. Years after her death, Royce's journal was published as *A Frontier Lady*.

CALIFORNIA, IN 1851.

BY SHIRLEY.

[THE following is the first of a series of letters, written by a lady who came to California in 1849, to her sister in "the States," as the land we left behind us was called at that time. They are penned in that light, graceful, epistolary style, which only a lady can fall into; and as they are a transcript of the impressions which the condition of California affairs, two years ago, made upon a cultivated mind, cannot fail to be of general interest.]

LETTER FIRST.

A TRIP INTO THE MINES.

Rich Bar, East Branch of the North Fork of Feather River,
September 13, 1851.

I CAN easily imagine, dear M——, the look of large wonder, which gleams from your astonished eyes, when they fall upon the date of this letter. I can figure to myself your whole surprised attitude, as you exclaim, "What in the name of all that is restless, has sent 'Dame Shirley' to Rich Bar?" How did such a shivering, frail, home-loving little thistle ever float safely to that far away spot, and take root so kindly, as it evidently has, in that barbarous soil? Where, in this living, breathing world of ours, lieth that same Rich Bar, which, sooth to say, hath a most taking name! And for pity's sake, how does the poor little fool expect to amuse herself there?"

Patience, sister of mine. Your curiosity is truly laudable; and I trust that before you read the postscript of this epistle, it will be fully and completely relieved. And first, I will merely observe *en passant*—reserving a full description of its discovery for a future letter—that said Bar forms a part of a mining settlement situated on the East Branch of the North Fork of Feather River, "away off up in the mountains," as our "little Faresoul" would say, at almost the highest point where, as yet, gold has been discovered, and indeed, within fifty miles of the summit of the Sierra Nevada itself. So much at present, for our *locale*, while I proceed to tell you of the propitious—or unpropitious as the result will prove—winds, which blew us hitherward.

You already know, that F——, after suffering for an entire year, with fever and ague, bilious, remittent, and intermittent fevers—this delightful list, varied by an occasional attack of jaundice,—was advised as a *dernier resort* to go into the mountains. A friend, who had just returned from the place, suggested Rich Bar, as the terminus of his health-seeking journey; not only on account of the extreme purity of the atmosphere, but because there were more than a thousand people there already, and but one physician; and as his strength increased, he might find in that vicinity a favorable opening for the practice of his profession, which, as the health of his purse was almost as feeble as that of his body, was not a bad idea.

F—— was just recovering from a brain fever, when he concluded to go to the mines; but in spite of his excessive debility, which rendered

VOL. I.   6

Letters Back Home

Another woman who went to the West was Louise Clappe. She followed her husband west in 1849. The trip by sea took five months and cost $300. Once she was in California, Clappe sent letters (shown left) to her sister Molly. In these letters, she described the hard work involved in mining. Her writing was also personal. She mentions the crude cabin in which they lived.

Grass Valley was a busy town during the Gold Rush.

Charley Parkhurst

Small, fringed gloves covered Charlotte Parkhurst's dainty hands. A pleated shirt hid her shapely figure. Who could have guessed that Parkhurst would be one of the greatest **stagecoach** drivers of all time?

As a young girl, Parkhurst ran away. She changed her name to Charley, and from that point on, she lived as a male. Parkhurst found work as a **groom**. The owner taught him how to care for horses and to drive wagons with more than one horse. In 1851, Parkhurst went to California. He drove stagecoaches for Wells Fargo and the California Stage Company.

Parkhurst once drove over a raging river moments before the bridge failed. He and the passengers made it just in time! Another time, a horse kicked him in the eye. After that, he wore a black eye patch.

Parkhurst died in his late 60s. That's when people found out that he was a woman. If the doctor hadn't told them, Parkhurst's friends wouldn't have believed it!

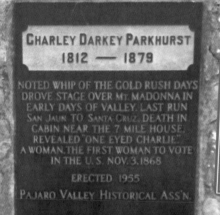

CHARLEY DARKEY PARKHURST
1812 — 1879

NOTED WHIP OF THE GOLD RUSH DAYS
DROVE STAGE OVER MT. MADONNA IN
EARLY DAYS OF VALLEY. LAST RUN
SAN JAUN TO SANTA CRUZ. DEATH IN
CABIN NEAR THE 7 MILE HOUSE.
REVEALED "ONE EYED CHARLIE"
A WOMAN. THE FIRST WOMAN TO VOTE
IN THE U. S. NOV. 3, 1868

ERECTED 1955

PAJARO VALLEY HISTORICAL ASS'N.

Voting Rights

In 1920, women won the right to vote in the United States. But Parkhurst was voting long before then. There is a plaque in Soquel, California, that marks the spot where some think he cast his vote in the 1868 election.

These men sit on the driver's bench of a stagecoach.

Mapping the West

John Charles Frémont was born in 1813 in Georgia. Even though he grew up in the South, he had a big effect on California. As a young boy, he was very good at math. He joined the United States Army in 1838. He became a mapmaker for the army. This skill would end up being very helpful when he mapped the huge, unknown lands of the West. The army sent Frémont on five trips to explore and map the new lands.

On his first trip, he met a guide named Christopher "Kit" Carson. Carson helped lead Frémont and his group through the South Pass. They quickly became friends. Frémont wrote about his trip and his opinion of the West. He believed the region was not dangerous and was ready to be settled. His stories and ideas made him very popular. Many people were inspired to travel to the West because of Frémont.

Kit Carson Peak

Rugged Mountain Man

Carson was an important explorer and guide in the West. He was a trapper, scout, and soldier. But it was the stories that Frémont wrote about him that made him a legend.

Carson and Frémont came to California on their second trip. Carson led the group through a new pass in the Sierra Nevada. Frémont named it *Carson Pass* in honor of his friend. The five trips would take Frémont to all different parts of the West. After each trip, he wrote about what he had learned, which helped change people's views of the West. Before his writings, many people thought the West was wild and dangerous. Frémont wrote that it had rivers and good soil for farming.

Frémont's reports became a handbook for people who wanted to go west. Most important were the maps that he created. Frontiersmen, like Carson, knew parts of the West very well. But they could not give good descriptions of where things were. Frémont was able to put all their thoughts together. People who read his stories wanted to move west. They studied his maps and followed them all the way to California.

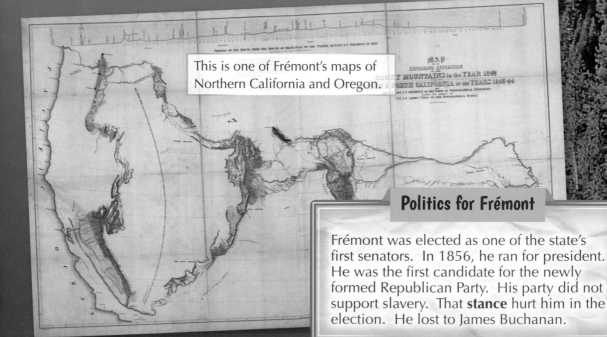

This is one of Frémont's maps of Northern California and Oregon.

Politics for Frémont

Frémont was elected as one of the state's first senators. In 1856, he ran for president. He was the first candidate for the newly formed Republican Party. His party did not support slavery. That **stance** hurt him in the election. He lost to James Buchanan.

Bear Flag Revolt

Frémont would later help plan and lead the Bear Flag Revolt. The Mexican-American War was declared in May 1846. News of the war did not reach the rebels. For three weeks, California was its own country! Frémont would later join the fight against Mexico.

Carson Pass

Paving the Way

Fur trappers, traders, and pioneers led the push to head west. They were lured by new prospects and wealth. So, they endured tough conditions as they led people westward. The trails they made can still be found today.

Thousands of miles of trails start in the Midwest and end in California. By the late 1800s, trains would become the main way to travel across the country. Later, major U.S. highways would be built along these same paths.

Despite these changes, hikers still flock to these early pioneer trails. Some of these trails are named after the people who **forged** them. The **legacies** of these people live on. For a long time, the West was a remote region that was almost impossible to reach. Thanks to these trailblazers, California was no longer a mystery. It was a place people wanted to visit. It was a place they wanted to call home.

Kit Carson Tree

In 1844, Carson was working as Frémont's guide. As they went over the Sierra Nevada, they stopped briefly to enjoy the view. They were 8,600 feet (2,621 meters) above sea level! Carson carved his name and the date on a tree in the area. This area would later be named *Kit Carson Pass*. The tree was cut down, but the section with his name was saved. It's stored in a museum.

Pack It!

Imagine that you are taking a trip by wagon to the West. You are traveling with your family, which includes you, your spouse, and two children, ages 6 and 10. You need supplies for everyone.

Remember, this trip will take around six months. You will be traveling during the heat of summer. You might also have to deal with cold, winter weather.

Organize your supplies into categories. What do you need to feed your family? What clothes are absolutely necessary? What supplies do you need for your children?

Glossary

cannibalism—the act of one human eating the body of another human

caretaker—a person who helps care for a person or place

crude—basic; rough

customs—traditional behaviors or actions of a group of people

debt—the state of owing an amount of money to someone

emigrants—people who leave a country or region to live elsewhere

fatigue—a feeling of being very tired

forged—formed or created something

groom—person who takes care of horses

gulches—narrow areas that streams run through

historians—people who write about or study history

huddled—sat closely together

industries—groups of businesses that provide products or services

legacies—things that happened or that come from people in the past

mission—an important task or job

paces—steps

party—a group of people who travel together

passes—routes that go through mountains so that people do not have to go around them

prospects—new opportunities

radical—very new and different from what is traditional

stagecoach—a horse-drawn, four-wheeled passenger wagon

stance—a publicly stated view or opinion

trappers—people who catch animals for their furs

underestimated—thought that something was less than the actual size or difficulty

unexcelled—unable to be bettered or topped

Index

Your Turn!

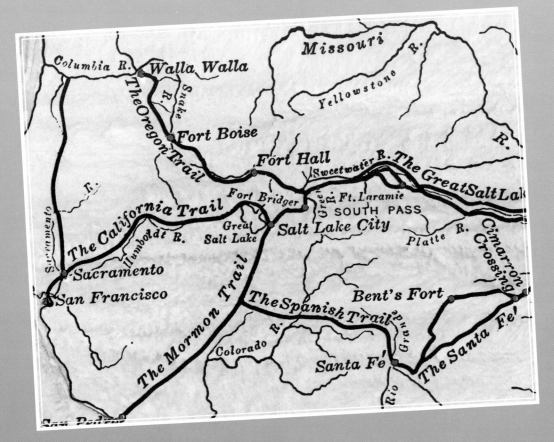

Trail Trek

Look at all the trails that led people to the West in the 1800s. Imagine you were traveling with your family at that time. Choose at least two trails. Write a paragraph describing the pros and cons of traveling on each one. Include which route would be better for your family to use and why.